WHIPTON

of Yesteryear

Chips Barber & Don Lashbrook

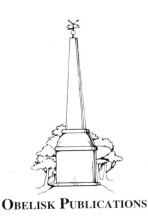

OBELISK PUBLICATIONS

OTHER TITLES IN THIS SERIES

Ashburton of Yesteryear, *John Germon and Pete Webb*
The Teign Valley of Yesteryear, Parts I and II, *Chips Barber*
Brixham of Yesteryear, Parts I, II and III, *Chips Barber*
Pinhoe of Yesteryear, Parts I and II, *Chips Barber*
Princetown of Yesteryear, Parts I and II, *Chips Barber*
Kingsteignton of Yesteryear, *Richard Harris*
Heavitree of Yesteryear, *Chips Barber*
Kenton and Starcross of Yesteryear, *Eric Vaughan*
Okehampton of Yesteryear, *Mike and Hilary Wreford*
Beesands and Hallsands of Yesteryear, *Cyril Courtney*
Exmouth of Yesteryear, *Kevin Palmer*
Sampford Peverell of Yesteryear, *Bridget Bernhardt & Jenny Holley*
Sidmouth of Yesteryear, *Chips Barber*
Lympstone of Yesteryear, Parts One and Two, *Anne Scott*
St Thomas of Yesteryear, Parts One and Two *Mavis Piller*
Ide of Yesteryear, *Mavis Piller*

OTHER TITLES ABOUT THIS AREA

The Lost City of Exeter – Revisited, *Chips Barber*
The Great Little Exeter Book, *Chips Barber*
An Alphington Album, *Pauline Aplin and Jeanne Gaskell*
The Ghosts of Exeter, *Sally and Chips Barber*
Exeter City – A File of Fascinating Football Facts, *Mike Blackstone*
Ian Jubb's Exeter Collection
Beautiful Exeter, *Chips Barber*
An Exeter Boyhood, *Frank Retter*
Exploring Exeter – The Heart of the City, *Jean Maun*
Exploring Exeter – The West Quarter, *Jean Maun*
Around the Churches of Exeter, *Walter Jacobson*
The Street-Names of Exeter, *Mary Ruth Raymond*

**We have over 170 Devon titles; for a full list please send an SAE to
Obelisk Publications, 2 Church Hill, Pinhoe, Exeter EX4 9ER**

**This book is dedicated to Peter Gentry
for all his good works for the community of Whipton**

Plate Acknowledgements
Thanks to Charles Radley for pictures on pages 14 to 19, 27 (bottom) and 29;
Mavis Piller for 30 (top) and Chips Barber for 30 (bottom)
All other pictures supplied by Don Lashbrook.

*First published in 2001 by
Obelisk Publications, 2 Church Hill, Pinhoe, Exeter, Devon
Designed and Typeset by Sally Barber
Printed in Great Britain*

WHIPTON *of Yesteryear*

This collection of pictures reveals a very different Whipton from the place we know today; many of the views featured are from an age when it was a village completely separate from Exeter. We begin our photographic journey back in time in what is now known as Whipton Village Road, an important through route in coaching days. The pale building towards the top left is the Half Moon Inn, now 'Micawbers'. Everything between it and the bottom right hand corner of the picture has disappeared, including one of the village's former post offices (with a horse and trap parked outside). This is now the pub's car park. Where the wall is seen, just below the Whipton Inn, is now the location of the Whipton Eye Centre. The picture below is similar but includes the opposite side of the street.

The two pictures on this page are looking in the opposite direction to the ones on the previous page. Above and below we are almost opposite the Whipton Inn and looking along the road towards the direction of Pinhoe. There were more thatched properties in the village at this time, when there was little more to Whipton than the buildings which lined the road through it. Certainly there was no need for pavements in those days!

The village's two pubs are featured in this pair of pictures. Here we have a group of smartly dressed regulars from the Half Moon ready to enjoy an outing to Princetown and Plymouth. The card on which this scene appeared was posted on 20 June 1925.

In the picture below we see the patrons of the Whipton Inn ready to enjoy a day out in the same era. Watching them leave is a dog leaning out from one of the pub's upstairs windows.

Whipton has had a number of post offices. Above is the first one, which stood close to the junction of Summer Lane and Whipton Village Road. Emily Payne, the lady in the centre of the trio, was postmistress for many years. Her husband, Sammy, was a blacksmith. At the time the photo was taken there were other Paynes living in this part of the road, then under the address of 'Lower Summerland'. Francis Payne lived at number 1 and was listed in the 1910 street directory as being a wagoner.

Whipton of Yesteryear

We have now moved a little further along the road. The sign on the wall, above the heads of the children on the left, says 'W H Payne, cycle agent', this being the building which became the second Whipton post office.

The picture below is amazing, as the foreground is now Pinhoe Road. This was built as a Whipton by-pass in the 1930s to relieve the growing amount of traffic passing through the village. On the right can be seen a footpath which led to All Saints Church from Hill Lane.

This is a close-up of what are now 50 and 52 Whipton Village Road, a combined and unexpectedly large newagents and electrical shop. This picture was taken in 1907 and features Winnie Payne when she was a babe-in-arms. Her home later became the second Whipton Post Office and is seen in both pictures on the opposite page. Below are All Saints Church and the former school, the latter built in 1871 on land given by Lord Poltimore. In 1938 the pupils moved to a new school; this building, which had served the community so well, was pulled down in 1969 to make way for a few houses.

Two similar views but taken in different years. Above shows us a low, single-storey building which is now the site of The Vet Centre. A sign on the wall, near the telephone kiosk, says 'Devon & Somerset Stores Ltd'. The card above was posted in June 1956.

Below, a Whiteway's Cyder lorry delivers to the Whipton Inn. A number of unattended bicycles and scooters are seen outside 'Shooter's', the shop with an awning seen to the left of the lorry.

Still in Whipton Village Road, the property with the three upstairs windows, at the end of the terrace and almost in the centre of the picture, is Rose Cottage. The gap beyond it is where Payne Court is now located. The picture postcard from which the view below was taken was posted by L. Shephard on 15 January 1907 to Miss Eveleigh of 6 Cholwell Cottages, Heavitree Bridge. The grocer's shop on the corner of Whipton Village Road, at the junction with Summer Lane, was run by Lucy and William Shephard at that time. For the record, they had two daughters, Florence ('Dolly') and Mabel. This view, similar to the one above, shows the gateway which led to Rowlands Farm.

Above we see the outside of All Saints Church and also its ornate altar. Below is its choir of 1900. The church became redundant at the end of the 1970s and St Boniface, in Brookway, took over the role of parish church. All Saints is now the Whipton Community Hall.

Dressed in their 'Sunday-Best', the children and teachers pose for the photographer, only one person partly obscuring her face.

Below and opposite it's party time, the people of Whipton getting into the right mood to enjoy the Coronation of George VI on 24 May 1937. The Whipton Inn can hardly be seen for the patriotic bunting, with most dressed up for the occasion. There is a cardboard cut-out of his majesty on the balcony and the pub has undergone a temporary change of name; that is, if the sign's to be believed.

The date given for the procession of the 'Whipton to London' coach is 12 May 1937, many Whiptonians turning out to see it trundle through the village.

The pictures on these two pages were all taken on 8 November 1963 and are from the family album of the late Charles Radley, as are those on the next four pages. They were kindly loaned by Mrs Fitzjohn, a local resident. Above, we look down towards the centre of the village; below and opposite we have several pictures of the junction of Summer Lane and Whipton Village Road when it was about to change its appearance …

Less than a year later, on 12 September 1964, this corner of the junction witnessed a major demolition job. These pictures show the different stages as the corner buildings, numbers 70 and 72, are taken down. No doubt the neighbouring windows required a good clean afterwards.

On this page we have two 1972 pictures, taken in opposite directions, of the eastern end of Whipton Village Road. These old cottages and Smithy have since been pulled down and replaced by 'new' houses. The stream, which caused the 'misery' shown in the three photos opposite, runs down the side of the road. This flood, caused by the Whipton Brook, was photographed on 30 September 1960. The top picture is an unseasonal Summer Close; the middle and bottom scenes are both in Summer Lane.

These two views are taken in drier weather. The one above shows a much more rural Whipton scene. Behind the pair of trees in the centre, and to the left of the barn, Whipton Halt, which opened in 1908 and closed in 1923, can be spied. The short platform begins just to the left of the left tree and continues behind it. A single person is waiting for the train. Below is a leafy Summer Lane.

Opposite are three photos of the Whipton Sanatorium, or 'Isolation Hospital', on the eastern side of Whipton, not far from where Sainsbury's store is today. It was built in 1878 and gives its name to Hospital Lane.

The quiet country village of Whipton, for that is exactly what it was in 1911, suddenly found itself the centre of more national attention. These marvellous pictures show scenes from the first Round Britain Air Race, when the 'Exeter Aviation Ground' was selected as one of the staging posts.

An Aviation Race Committee was formed and the site was deemed to be ideal. As the local press stated: *The great topic of the week has been the great race by the airmen. The local control being so near, the whole parish seemed to take the opportunity of catching a glimpse of the wonderful machines and their drivers, and on Tuesday evening and Wednesday morning a large portion of the population might have been found within a few hundred yards of Whipton village. The interest aroused for two or three days was really surprising. It was nothing else but aeroplanes; they were 'in the air' in more ways than one. I suppose for most people it was the first time they had seen an aeroplane, and then, again, we are not likely to see any more this way for a bit ...*

The organising committee zoned off the ground into five areas and even went to the trouble of installing a telephone. Most spectators were obliged to walk to the 'air-field'; some arrived by horse-drawn carriage but the better-off came by car. Zone A was the place to be for the best view of the planes, where a shilling (5p) bought a close-up of the action.

En route to Exeter Samuel Franklin Cody's big machine, nicknamed 'Cody's Cathedral', struggled with the unfavourable conditions. He made an overnight stop, choosing to land on the wide expanse of Weston-super-Mare's beach. Although Cody (1862–1913) had a telegram sent to tell of his delay, it never reached Whipton; whilst the crowd expectantly watched the skies for his arrival he was busy giving a speech in the Somerset resort.

The start of the race was delayed because of strong winds; these flimsy flying machines, 'of bicycle-frame tubing, bamboo, wire and canvas, and fitted with motor car engines and wooden propellers', were hardly equipped to cope with extremes of weather. Apart from the use of obvious features of the landscape, such as railways and broad rivers, the planes were navigated by compass. Pilots must have dreaded fog or low cloud; indeed, many of those forced to land were obliged to ask directions on which way to proceed. In the race seventeen of the planes suffered engine problems. The race was intended to take place on 27–28 July but went on for some days longer as pilots, hit by a range of set-backs, eventually straggled home. A close was put on after twelve days.

There was a major incentive to win the race; the first prize of £10,000 was an extraordinary amount in those days. The *Daily Mail* sponsored the prize but there wasn't an official second prize; it was all or nothing. However, a further £200 was later raised for the gallant runner-up. Mr Valentine – shown above and opposite, top left and bottom – had an eventful time along the way, including a forced landing when a valve rod broke. When news reached Whipton that Mr Valentine was on his way a large crowd gathered to greet him. Because he was coming from Bristol most cast their gaze towards Pinhoe Church, assuming that this would be his direction of approach. However, he came in from the direction of the city, having followed the Great Western line all the way to St David's before heading out along the Waterloo line to Whipton. He was the first Englishman home and received a fine gold cup. He was given a great reception by the Town Clerk, Sheriff (Sir James Owen) and Mayor (Mr A. T. Loram), who took him off to the New London Inn for a slap-up breakfast before he carried on his journey in his Deperdumin monoplane.

The winner of the 1010-mile-long race was Mr Beaumont (shown top right on page 24), a Lieutenant in the French Navy. Second place went to to Mr Vedrines, another Frenchman. This is how the press reported their progress: *The leaders had been expected at Exeter on Tuesday and thousands of people had made their way to the alighting ground at Whipton. Visitors came from all parts of the county and all the roads in the vicinity were thronged. Late in the evening the crowds dissolved, but some elected to stay for the night in the fields or hedgerows ... Those who went home did so with the determination to return the first thing in the morning, for the planes were expected about 4 am, and long before daybreak there was another exodus from the city. Special trains from Queen-steet and special trams to Pinhoe-road helped swell the mass, and by 5 o'clock from ten to fifteen thousand people were on the watch. Only a small proportion of them were in the field itself, where the takings (including £35 on Tuesday) were £162. Just after 6 o'clock, and after several false alarms, general cheering announced the appearance of the first machine, and in a very short space Vedrines swung round by Pinhoe Church tower, at a height of about 1500 feet, and brought his plane down swiftly, landing beautifully. But before that the spectators had had one of the finest sights of the whole circuit - two planes high in the air, within a quarter of a mile of each other, sailing a third of a mile above the earth as serenely as a pair of seagulls. Beaumont on the second machine, who landed two minutes after Vedrines, was well in front of him on flying time. Vedrines was obviously worried, and said little; Beaumont was affable and all smiles.*

Above, the Bath & West Show took place at Whipton in 1909. Gray's, a firm which had specialist camping shops in Exeter for many years, were present, as the flag and tent on the left show. The venue was later used for the annual Devon County Show until, cramped for space and parking, in 1989 it moved out to Westpoint, Clyst St Mary, where a much bigger site has been developed.

Below, it's late August 1961 and we are back in the centre of Whipton, seeing more change at the junction of Pinhoe Road and Hill Lane.

The lanes in the vicinity of the village have changed almost beyond recognition. On this page we have two views looking along the lane past the former Whipton Barton Farm, farmed by the Alfords until the 1950s, and the nearby Stone's Cottages. The top picture looks away from the village, the lower one towards it.

On the opposite page three photos taken on 6 November 1963 show Whipton Barton just before it was demolished.

Whipton of Yesteryear

There are many shops either side of Polsloe Bridge: some are in Whipton, but these are in the parish of St Mark's. The post office still trades but with a change of emphasis, as for many years it doubled up as a wool shop. The message on the card, posted to Neasden, London NW 10 on 26 September 1954, said 'Just a reminder of where the wool for Aunt Alice's cardigan was purchased!' The shop to its right, F. R. Snell, later became the colourful Merv Hutchings' shop, selling all sorts of industrial and work-wear clothing. At one time this late entrepreneur had warehouse premises near Exeter Quay. The shop on the far right, then 'Newton the Grocer', later became premises for Roman Glass. Out of picture to the right of this is the Pinhoe Road Baptist Church. Below is a relatively modern picture showing Whipton Wools at 358 Pinhoe Road shortly before it closed. In January 1998 it reopened as a Sue Ryder charity shop.

There was a time when there were houses on one side only of a much narrower, almost traffic-free Pinhoe Road. Here we stand near Polsloe Bridge looking uphill towards Mount Pleasant. The shop on the right, now an off-licence, was listed in 1910 as being 'Wills Bros, grocers and provision dealers'.

The picture below is much later and also looks uphill, the tower of St Mark's Church making an obvious landmark.

Depending on your direction of travel, Polsloe Bridge is the gateway either into or out of Whipton. The picture below was taken from the former eastern platform of Polsloe Bridge Halt, looking towards Whipton. The filling station on the left has also since disappeared. There are now traffic lights at the junction with Beacon Lane and a bus lane beyond where the double-decker, a City of Exeter green-and-cream bus, overtakes a parked vehicle. This was taken in those idyllic days when motoring, and even parking, was a joy!